CHANGE THE WORLD

MY ULTIMATE TRAINING GUIDE

MARK A.J. DICKINSON

Published by markdickinson.com
Cover image produced using Canva
Information about the publisher
www.markdickinson.com

Available for companies and in quantity for bulk
purchases and learning

Dedicated to those who seek excellence.
100% Happy Customers
100% of the Time

CONTENTS

CHAPTER ONE
INTRODUCTION

I can change the world - one person at a time.

Sitting in the living room of our home I was just 14 when my older sister was attending her Train the Trainer program at work, and she had to practise what she was learning, so she asked me to be her trainee. I loved it. She taught me how to set up a breakfast tray and I was hooked. My sister was an Executive Housekeeper in hotels and she was really good at it. She even won an award from Trusthouse Forte as the Housekeeper of the Year runner up and my mom and I got to attend the ceremony and this got me more interested. My sister let me help her during my school break and I was allowed to collect the dirty linen from the beds and take it to the laundry. Well for me, this was a lot of fun and I fell in love with the hospitality industry. I took all of my school choices for hospitality and just two years later I left school and went to a local college in my hometime to become a chef; but the college had other ideas, they had just started a management course and I was selected to be in that course instead of the chef course. I loved everything about it (except food science) and was determined to be a hotel manager. I left college on a Friday at the end of the second year and started work on the following Monday as a trainee manager for a hotel chain called De Vere Hotels.

And work it was. Each day was very long. We worked in the coffee shop serving breakfast, took a short break and then worked in an admin department of the hotel during the morning, at lunch we were back in the coffee shop and then in the evening we worked in the restaurant. There was a stint in every department, in the kitchen, the cellar, bars, banqueting and conferences, housekeeping, front office, reception, the switchboard (they no longer exist) and finally in the management office. After almost two years of working 16 hours a day (we lived in the hotel so arriving to work was instant) I got promoted to an assistant manager in the Queen's Hotel in Eastbourne and it was here that I was selected to attend Train the Trainer. I was fascinated by training but did not truly understand its power to change people's behavior and set a course for excellence. About a year in I was selected to attend an advanced Train the Trainer course and was certified as a trainer and a planner of training.

My journey from there took me to my home country of Scotland where I worked at the prestigious Gleneagles Hotel and the doors to luxury hotels were swung wide open. The people I met were magical; there were royal family members, film stars, famous people and at that time four golf courses, a riding school and the Jackie Stewart Shooting School, where I learned to become pretty handy at skeet shooting.

My dream was to travel the world and my next move took me to Shanghai in the late 1980's and then on to Uganda in East Africa. In Uganda we were the President's chosen hotel for all state banquets and as an Assistant Food & Beverage Manager I had the opportunity to meet and greet many heads of state from around the world, including Nelson Mandella. My career and dreams were unfolding in wonderful ways and my next move took me to Kanchanaburi in Thailand, where I was part of the opening team as Food & Beverage Manager. This led to me being taken on as Food & Beverage Director of the Royal Orchid in Bangkok where we had 770 rooms and 8 food and beverage outlets and banqueting for up to 1000 people. We claimed the award as the best city hotel in the world two years in a row and I was flying. I built an academy within the hotel, focused on training and growing my team of 450 employees and I began to use the training skills from my earlier years. I distinctly remember going to the General Manager one day and asking him for his expectations of what I should be doing and he simply replied, "That's what we hired you for". Carte blanche. I was in my element.

My journey continued to The Tokyo American Club in Japan where I became Director of Food & Beverage Operations and it was there that I created an orientation program for the entire team that was linked to customer happiness. It was very successful and became the foundation for all that has followed.

I left Japan for the Middle East and have been in this region ever since. My family is based in Beirut and I have worked in many of the Middle Eastern countries opening restaurants, running restaurants, and building training programs. During that time I moved into mass participation events, operating the Beirut International Marathon as its General Manager and then I launched my first company, Ideaz Factory. We did everything, which was both good and bad. We mainly focused on training but I also had a TV show for entrepreneurs which aired on local TV. That was a lot of fun too. During that period I started a software company for measuring customer happiness and employee happiness, but it needed a lot of funds and I was not yet experienced enough in running my own business to sustain it, so I returned to my roots and was CEO for a couple of restaurant chains in the Middle East and then again in Thailand.

It was during this period that I recognized the need for training in the hospitality industry and decided to create a software that would manage training for restaurants. And, as they say, the rest is history. The company is called Done.fyi, the name was designed around the concept that once you have built your learning platform you are done and the FYI was a joke, for your information! Today we have thousands of users around the world and everything we do is to improve people's lives through training, learning and growth.

My favorite program to train is Train the Trainer. Watching the transformation of managers through this program gives me the greatest pleasure in everything that I do. We have a team based in the UAE and we operate our platform in many countries around the world, many of them being in the Middle East.

I hope that as you read this book you will learn how to create outstanding training programs that inspire others to strive for excellence and that you will be instrumental in growing the professionalism of managers within our industry.

Keep this one thought in mind, "I can change the world - one person at a time". It just takes one person to have that thought and we have already begun the process.

I will be the one.

CHAPTER TWO
WHY TRAINING MAKES SENSE

Training is the first pillar of excellence.

Through training you take the dreams and foundational thoughts of an owner and convert them into living action within an operation. Commencing with hand washing through to serving customers exactly as was originally intended, everything is a learning experience.

Take nothing for granted. What you know, you learned. You either absorbed it by watching someone else do it, you were taught it, or you discovered through trial and error. In all cases, at some point you did not know what you now know. We must never take for granted that our team members know what we want them to do. We must explicitly and carefully explain exactly what we want them to do, however this is time consuming and requires patience to build the right material.

When you think about it, building any kind of operation requires a large capital investment and this is actioned after a lot of thought. Planning and design, construction, team selection, menu design, operational planning and opening are all immersive skills that develop a unique offering for customers. The challenge arises once the operation opens, for it is in this activity that we discover that people are not always as clear on what we expect of them as we had at first imagined. Heavy pre-opening training programs are common and then remedial training to develop the team to produce the standards required. What happens next is the common challenge to our entire industry, and that is to rely upon the team to teach new joiners what we want. As we all know, salaries of new joiners are at the lower end of the scale, as are the skills and it is often assumed that they will learn as they go along. This is a fallacy. They will learn only what they need to know to perform their role, but not necessarily the meaning behind it. This puts the capital investment at the risk of being reduced to zero by a front line team member who has not been shown how to do their job, not taught why they are doing it and not yet skilled in delivering exceptional service experiences.

Every time an employee does not know an answer to a customer question, the reputation takes a small hit. The value of the business is depreciated. When employees don't know the products that they are serving, or the ingredients in a product, they are reducing the value of the business. When these front line employees are not taught how to speak eloquently with customers or the style of the operation, they are reducing the investment value. All of this happens out of the spotlight, unseen by management. It is the micro transactions between a busboy and a waiter in front of a customer that makes a negative impact on customers. All of this makes the investment value fall and causes customers to silently leave. On the contrary, customers very quickly sense excellence and professionalism from service team members and reward your business in amazing ways. They talk about you, they bring friends and they spend more. They share about you online and become your best marketing plan.

So, with this in mind, protecting the investment, training becomes the top priority of every manager. In my opinion, the greatest managers are able to do nothing during service, for they have trained their team to perform excellently, to deliver the standards required and to make beautiful memorable experiences for customers.

By now I imagine you are wondering why I use the word Customer and not Guest, here's why: a customer pays for a service based upon your offering, and they have the expectation that you will either live up to your offering, or hopefully exceed it. Guests are people that are invited with no financial link. When you visit my home, you are my guest. There is no check at the end of your visit and you will be delighted by the various activities and services that you receive in my home. If I fall short of your expectation in some way, you will not harm me, though you may relate the story to your friends, generally it will pass. A customer however is going to pay for my services and they expect value for money. No matter what the establishment may call their customers, it could be clients or guests, there is a disconnect between what we call them and what they are expecting. Customers deserve the best return on their investment of time and money in coming to our business and we are here to ensure that they get it. An excellent product served poorly becomes a poor experience. An average product served excellently becomes a good experience. Keeping the idea that these are my customers causes me to be more vigilant about their expectations and inspires me to do my best to do as much as possible to surpass their expectations.

We must destroy the myth of guest satisfaction. It is a dangerous path to mediocrity and denies us the opportunity of becoming the best in our field. The first step is to understand the meaning of satisfaction. To be satisfied is to feel an equilibrium or balance between what we are paying and what we received. If the balance is there we experience satisfaction. When there is an imbalance to the negative, we experience disappointment, frustration or even anger. When the imbalance is on the positive side we experience happiness and delight.

If we convert these ratings into numbers we end up with something like Net Promoter Score (NPS). My scale looks like this:

HAPPINESS SCALE

10	Happiness	
9	Very good	Positive zone
8	Good	
7	Average	Zero impact zone
6	Not bad	Negative zone
5	Poor	
4	Disappointing	
3	Frustrating	
2	Anger	
1	Utterly miserable	

Looking at the scale you will see that good and average are rated at 7 to 8. This translates into a 4 star rating out of 5. To be very good and above you must score at least 9 and above or 4.5 on the star rating chart.

As I am sure you already know, this is extremely difficult to do and requires great focus. The great operations that win the awards and that stand out above all the others are those that attain 9 and above. NPS states that the score of 7 & 8 is actually worth 0 to your business. Customers who rate 7 & 8 do not do anything for you, either negative or positive. They don't promote you and they may or may not return. It was just another average or good experience. If the offering was rated below 7 you are in the negative zone. What this means for your business is that if your customers are rating you below a 9 or 4.5, everything you are doing is for nothing.

You have wasted all your capital investment and energy to deliver a 0 or worse, and to my mind that is the worst thing that can happen to your business.

In this life we are overwhelmed with the choices of hospitality locations that we can go to. It is essential that we score above 9 and to do that we must aim higher than 9 so that if and when we fall short, we will remain in the positive zone. That leaves us just one option, aim for 10.

If every manager in our industry was obsessed with being a 10, the standards would immediately begin to rise. We would see our business as a whole improve. It is imperative that you grasp this concept and then convert it into action.

How do we become focused on 10? Decide that it is our only standard.

Everyone can be a 10!

You can be a 10.

But you must decide now that this is what you want to be. If you are not ready to be a 10 then you probably won't get much out of the rest of this book because you are not ready to do the hard work. If you are desperate to be a 10, obsessed with the idea of being 10 and demand that your entire team walk that journey, then you are in the right place.

What I am sharing in this book is how to be the best of the best, not one of, but the One.

To be a 10 there are some very important foundational blocks that must be in place and none are more important than ensuring that you have built a business where employees can be happy, for it is happy employees that make happy customers.

Happy employees = Happy customers

Happy employees are those that are rewarded fairly, listened to, respected and above all trained. If you take care of my needs, you are willing to let me speak when I have something to say, you respect my commitment to your organisation and you show me how to do what you want me to, then I will be happy. It sounds so basic and simple, and yet it is ignored by many.

Stop building empires and towering hierarchies. Build simple organisational structures that make sense, conserve resources and empower those that actually serve customers. When there is a Director of Operations, a General Manager and an Assistant General Manager and then a Floor Manager, Supervisors and finally the Service Team, we have overcooked it. The possibility of the Director ever hearing the truth of what is required at the sharp end is severely impeded. By nature we like to look good in front of others, and so we filter. When the structure empowers team members and trusts them to do their jobs, and there are good systems in place, then we have an organisation capable of being a 10, simply because communication can be free and easy and the senior manager is close to the team that are serving customers without layers in the way, filtering the real and important messages. It keeps costs down too, for every title comes at a price and by reducing the number of layers to the absolute minimum, you increase operational efficiency.

Simple is beautiful.

Why training makes sense is because it is focused on the perceivable value of a service transaction and in elevating that experience to the highest level. Training makes sense because it assures the accurate, recorded knowledge transfer from someone who knows and empowers someone who must know. Training makes sense because it engages team members and provides them with the power to learn their work at onset of their employment and it empowers and inspires them to grow as they pursue their career in the business, lowering turnover and increasing performance, productivity and building trust.

Every penny invested in training will return multiple times over in outstanding customer experiences.

I hear - I forget

I see - I remember

I do - I understand

This is an age old statement that encapsulates the entire training process for me and has become one of my mantras. If i tell you, the chances of you remembering are very low. If I show you, I increase your probability of remembering what I have said, and if I can get you to do it, then I will be certain that you have understood what it is I want you to do. The power in this statement is that it engages the learner's brain on three different levels, auditory, visual and kinesthetic, and by using all three ways we trigger the brain's ability to retain information. Each person learns differently so by engaging all three ways we increase the probability of creating long term memories, which are important for making learning long lasting.

CHAPTER 3
WHAT MUST BE TRAINED

Everything.

You must train people on everything. There are no shortcuts, there is no easy way out or magic trick to make it done, however this book will help you if you follow the chapter titles and the Basic Sessions to Include in Key Roles *Appendix 1* where we have put together our top list of most important sessions for key roles within hospitality. They number somewhere around 250 sessions at this point in time, and we continue to add more roles and more sessions as we discover what is most used by our customers in their academies.

Your objective is to build an academy that fits your operation. The word Academy sounds good, and feels good for team members. It gives a sense of organisation and strength to incoming team members and is a source of pride for those who create their own academy. We build on the foundation that the system will run the business and people will run the system. This means that the system is no longer dependent upon an individual being present and neither upon a bunch of documents held by one individual, but rather a library of information that is freely available to all team members for the role that they occupy and for their areas of responsibility.

Systems run restaurants
People run systems

What must be trained is discovered through a process called training needs analysis and there are many ways that you can arrive upon the content. The first and most important way is to work through the process of onboarding a new employee into the company, then into each department and then each section and then finally into each role.

This instantly provides a form of clarity and structure that is simple and logical to follow, and this is set out in the chapters of this guide.

A common way that operations identify training needs is through mystery shoppers. However we avoid having mystery shoppers for a number of reasons, primarily because these are outsiders who are paid for their ability to identify issues, but in our opinion this causes a conflict, being paid to find problems can result in distracting from the original purpose of identifying real service issues and get lost on things that don't always add value to the customer experience. Secondly, the mystery shoppers do not know or usually have access to our proprietary intellectual property, meaning our standards and way of operating. Therefore we prescribe a system called Sit & Watch®. In this 2 hour process we recommend that team members experience the operation on the busiest days and are required to act as a customer. They will experience the service and take notes throughout. The reason they are required to do it on the busiest of days is that they will see the most deviations from the standards. Team members know the standards intimately and are able to figure out logical solutions to the problems that they discover and then recommend the appropriate training to resolve the issues found. It is a bold move and one that yields outstanding results, builds trust amongst the team members and rewards team members in the process. For more on Sit & Watch® get in touch with us and we will share the full process.

Further training needs are discoverable through a variety of useful tools:

Breakage reports

Wastage reports

Accident reports

Live customer comments

Online feedback

Employee comments and suggestions

Employee performance reviews

Career Succession

The objective of these tools is to highlight any task that can be improved or modified to eliminate the occurrence of a deviation from standards and to assure good processes are constantly being added to your Academy.

The process for building your Academy is akin to building a master matrix of material that is broken down by department and role. This matrix is best managed through an online learning platform (of course we would recommend that you use DONE) where you have a full list of every task to be learned by every job role and a method to record that these tasks have been trained and then to measure individuals' performance against those tasks.

This requires detailed planning and execution. Frequently the WHAT is clearly identified, but the process of getting everyone up to standard becomes complex and difficult to manage. Through our process, you will be able to do this seamlessly and hold everyone in the hierarchy accountable for their part.

It has been said that Proper Planning Prevents Poor Performance, another mantra that we stand by.

PPPPP

Training attracts many acronyms but this one is worth remembering. Sir Winston Churchill famously said, "Failure to plan is planning to fail".

The power of a training matrix is that you create records of training completed and you are able to accurately measure the performance of every individual against a realistic and tangible list of tasks. The matrix eliminates moodiness and creates defined and specific learning that is important.

Our objective is to train every person on everything that they will need to know in order to perform their role to the highest standard as defined by the company.

CHAPTER FOUR
WHO MUST BE TRAINED AND WHEN

Everyone.

Everyone must be trained, from the CEO to the front line employees, without exception. Everyone must be part of a learning process and the learning must firstly be appropriate to their position and secondly cause ongoing learning. When we stop learning, we mentally die. You already know the saying, "We cannot solve the problem with the same level of thinking that we were at when we created those problems" (Albert Einstein), and so it is beholden unto us to grow and learn for the rest of our lives, ensuring that we will evolve to better problem solving and higher ways of thinking. This involves being in a learning process and the best way to ensure this happens is to create one.

Our goal is to ensure that every single person in our organisation is learning and growing as this will ensure that our business is constantly improving. By building your Academy you commit your team to lifelong learning, and we believe that can only be a good thing!

The second part of our title is WHEN?

The simple answer is, "All the time".

Training must be an ongoing, constant process where the spirit of learning is instilled into every team member. Training is a journey with no end. With each step we become aware of the possibilities of further growth, and with the newly gained knowledge we are able to create material for developing individuals to the next level.

Our objective is to have every person in our organisation learning and growing all the time.

The cost benefits to this process are immeasurable. Once we have a reliable system in place we are able to focus our hiring process on finding the best possible entry level team members who will, by time, and through learning, become our future leaders. It is inspiring and motivating for team members to see that their future opportunities lie within the business, and this helps build trust and commitment and further reduces the need to leave to grow.

CHAPTER FIVE
WHO SHOULD TRAIN

ME!

The most important element of a successful Academy is personal commitment to training from the most senior people in the organisation. Conducting training is fun, exciting and rewarding and again, inspires the team that even their most senior managers are knowledgeable and capable to train.

A trainer must know the material from first hand experience and be able to communicate their knowledge first hand. They must be passionate about sharing that knowledge to their team and understand how to do it effectively and efficiently. Our aim is that through this book you will be able to do this.

Having created the library of knowledge the challenge is to transfer this knowledge to all of the team members. Secret information is useless. Many people in our industry are afraid to share their knowledge with others because they feel that it threatens their security or usefulness. This is just not true. When it comes to secrecy, recipes are a topic that I often face. Here's my take on this: your recipe is a list of ingredients and a method that works in your establishment. What the recipe does not share is the actual supplier of the ingredients, this is your secret. Just select any recipe at random from your list of recipes and type it into Google and you will find millions of results, at the end it is not about your recipe, it's about your supply chain and your presentation.

Commit to being a part of training for the rest of your life.

Make time to train at least once per month. Show people what you expect and you, as a talented leader will be able to give more life and texture to the training session than anyone else. You know better than everyone how things should be done and what you expect, so roll up your sleeves and get stuck in.

Knowledge + Experience = Able

CHAPTER SIX
WHERE TO TRAIN

There are two main types of training, On The Job and Off The Job.

OTJ, as it is frequently called, is conducted in the place of work. It is conducted in smaller groups with a team or an individual with a specific skill in mind. We recommend that a training season for a particular task be broken down into a 30 minute live session. This gives sufficient time to train one task, and is easily fitted into a daily training program. It ensures that the excuse of no time to train is eliminated. Remember, the more we train our team members on how to do their job and explain what is expected, the less time we need to spend supervising them and correcting errors or solving problems. Well trained team members produce excellent work, allowing us more time for other activities.

OTJ should be conducted in a part of the working environment where team members have access to all the required materials and where they feel comfortable. Find a place with the least distractions and ensure that phones are only used where required for signing in to training sessions and for tasks related to training. Make sure your own phone is set to silent or given to someone outside of the training session who can handle any calls while you are conducting the session.

Make it clear where the training session is going to take place and be there at least five minutes before. Avoid having trainees in the group who may be called upon to provide service to customers.

Off The Job Training happens away from the workplace and is suitable for knowledge training. In this case prepare the room, coffee breaks, lunches and materials well in advance and communicate the time and place well beforehand. Ensure that you provide sufficient time throughout the program to allow the participants to catch up with calls and follow up during breaks. Off the Job Training tends to be longer in nature and requires extended focus from participants, and so it is your responsibility to cater for this need by providing nice things like good coffee, bites and snacks as well as candy and even giveaways. Make sure that you check out the venue well in advance too, to ensure that the venue will allow the kind of interaction that you are looking for. Good lighting and an excellent sound system are essential and make sure to have sufficient flipcharts for teams to work together and produce interesting results.

CHAPTER SEVEN
CREATING CONTENT FOR TRAINING

Content creation is a skill that can be learned.

To create content we must know the desired outcome of the session and this requires specific and detailed knowledge and experience on the topic. Training something you don't know is normally a recipe for disaster because someone will call you out on the material and you will not be able to answer them.

Start by considering the desired outcome for your session:

By the end of this session what will they be able to do?
By the end of this session what will they know?

This will guide us in our preparation.

Research the topic. Even if you know the subject well, go to the internet and research it again. Never copy paste. Training evolves, techniques change, systems improve and so as we prepare for a training session we must keep in mind our ultimate objective: having the trainees able to do what we want them to do or to know what we want them to know.

This sounds basic, but without planning your content and then reviewing it before training you will not be able to deliver a comprehensive and complete session.

Here's a great way to create sessions:

1. Create a title for the session.
2. Focus on creating content for a specific role and task - keeping in mind who the trainee will be and keeping the content at their level
3. Write out the standards for this session.
4. Add examples of what the standards look and sound like.
5. Break the standards down into small pieces, chunks or blocks
   > Point 1, Point 2, Point 3...
   > Step 1, Step 2, Step 3...
   > A, B, C...

Limit the number of pieces of content to around 5 per session. This will work really well. Your job in creating a session is creating a pattern that people can learn, and retain. In order to do this you must be aware of how the brain stores the information that you are training.

The brain has three levels of memory. Short term, working and long term, and in order for our session to succeed we need to enable the learners to move the information into their long term storage.

> **Short term memory** - last seconds - initial response to data and screening it for value and importance.
>
> **Working memory** - lasts 10 to 20 mins (souza 2001) and retains 7 pieces (plus or minus 2) of information (Miller's Law 1956)
>
> **Long term memory** - lasts extensively and is available for retrieval - long term memories will be enhanced by follow up and repetition after the session.

As you put the session together you want to ensure that you keep in mind the following ways of enhancing the learning process:

Repetition - getting learners to repeat the information/process

Elaboration - explain it in detail and get them to explain it too

Organisation - organised information is easier to store - so make the steps logical and well organised

Storage - use hearing/listening, showing and doing (Auditory, Visual and kinesthetic) to build blocks to causing long term memories of the information

Breaks - ensure that the session is contained within the 30 minute time zone. Optimal learning is no longer than 40 minutes, so by creating sessions that fall well within this frame you will encourage learning. Breaks allow the mind to absorb what has just been learned before you move on to another topic.

Create a good way to help learners to remember the lesson that you want them to retain. This must work for you and your learners. Here are three ways that I believe work extremely well.

Acronyms - I am sure you are familiar with the acronym TEAM - **T**ogether **E**veryone **A**chieves **M**ore. This is a method of creating memory tools that enhance retention of information.

Mnemonics - a sentence or word string that associates words to the learning - **R**ichard **of Y**ork **G**ained **B**attles **I**n **V**ain helps us to remember the colours of the rainbow, Red, Orange, Yellow, Green, Blue, Indigo, Violet.

NLP (Neuro-linguistic programming) - Changing someone's thoughts or desires to achieve a desired result - There are limitless ways of using NLP and in order to do so, one must first study it deeply, then practise it. A simple technique from NLP that is very effective in helping to memorise is anchoring. A simple way of using anchoring is to elevate the state of the trainees through a breathing exercise, standing up or similar and then have them repeat the acronym or mnemonic out loud together. This will assist learners to memorise the points.

In creating content keep in mind that it should be:
- Interesting
- Valuable
- Attention grabbing
- Create connections between this session and what they may already know
- Involve practice/practical application

The content creation process is time consuming and detailed. By having the title, the standards and the learning blocks we are now ready to construct the session, so here it is:

My Training Session Content
- Session Title
- Who its for
- Why it is being trained and the desired outcome
- The standard or topic to be trained, written out in detail
- The learning blocks for learning this standard

Now you have figured out the content creation process you are ready to get started with building awesome training sessions and programs.

CHAPTER EIGHT
MISSION, VISION & VALUES

There are thousands of books on the subject of Mission, Vision and Values, or MVV as I like to call them, and I am not here to add another tome to the pile. In this chapter I want to cover what is essential for your team members to know and not really work on the construction of the MVV.

As we consider the employee journey into the workplace the very first thing that we want them to know is WHY we exist and this can be found in the Vision of the company. The second things is WHAT we are here to do, which is the mission and finally our BELIEFS, which are discovered through our values.

The MVV must be boldly communicated to our team right at the outset so that they are crystal clear on what kind of organisation they have joined, why it exists and what they are participating in.

We should have a statement that tells our team members the overall Vision for the business, where it is going in the long term. This will inspire employees to stay longer and commit to the big picture thinking.

Knowing the mission will clarify what it is we are here to do and create a common understanding between all team members of the desired outcome of our efforts.

Finally the values will be listed, with a brief description of what each value actually means within the company.

MVV is a first day exercise for every team member within any serious organisation. In our platform (DONE) we have a spot reserved for the MVV that comes before any other session, and we will mention it again in our chapter on the Orientation training program.

Displaying the MVV in a beautiful visual way will make the content memorable. You can also come back to this content again later with a training session on the Mission Vision and Values… what is essential is to have this high value information easily available to every team member, and to reference it as often as possible through all the training sessions that follow, so that there is a consistency of messaging and communication that is in alignment with the content.

No mission? No direction!

CHAPTER NINE
EMPLOYEE HANDBOOK

A great employee handbook is essential yet infrequently found. Most often it is a project under construction, which is absolutely fine. We believe that you should take whatever handbook you have right now and share it with your team, and keep on developing it as you discover what you need to add. The advantage of sharing what you already have is that the employees will have a go-to place to get general information and their questions about things that are not contained therein will guide you to knowing what to create next.

The employee handbook is not training so much as providing a resource, a go to place, a wiki, so that you reduce the amount of communication about basic things.

There are templates for employee handbooks in abundance and there are common basics that are included in every handbook so putting one together is not an impossible task, just a time consuming one.

We include the handbook at the front end of training with the hope that every team member will be shown where to find the help they need in times of conflict, trouble or doubt or where to get answers to their structure questions.

The tone of the handbook must be in alignment with the values. If one of your values is constant learning and acceptance of mistakes, then the handbook has to clearly show that the company has a process for remedial action that recovers people from mistakes without punishing them.

Make it available to everyone at any time. Remember? No secrets!

We will mention this again in our chapter on the Orientation Training Program.

CHAPTER TEN
JOB DESCRIPTION

Job descriptions have long been secret documents held by HR. This is clearly not a good idea. Tell people what they are here to do and the chances of them doing it will immediately increase.

Job descriptions are a compass for an employer and an employee

We must first determine the work required of our business, then break that work down into job roles that are appropriate to our organisation.

Once we have the hierarchy the excitement begins. Writing job descriptions is very important to the training process, for the job description is going to guide the employee hired to do the job, their supervisor and the trainer.

- The employee will have a clear document detailing for them what they are here to do.
- The supervisor will know exactly what is required of their team members in each role.
- The trainer will be able to ensure that there is training for every aspect of the job role in every position.

We recommend that JD's are very simple and to the point, use the minimum number of words possible to communicate. Avoid anything that is vague or ambiguous and avoid anything that is not measurable.

We always like to add the qualities of the person in this role. This has great benefits. Firstly it requires the creator of the JD to think about what kind of person they want to have in the business, and these qualities must align with the values of the company. Secondly they inspire the employee receiving the JD to believe themselves into those qualities, for example: Brave is a quality of a person in this role. Translate: We hired you because you are brave. Action on the floor? Courageous employees!

Tell them they are awesome and they will become so!

Every job can be summed up in about twenty five words. Here's what your job is for: Make 100% happy customers, 100% of the time and be profitable. Spend time to whittle down all the words that you want to write and keep just the absolute minimum. Make it as tight as possible and simple to memorise. You could make it as simple as "Excellently deliver the company Mission".

I said this was exciting, and if you do it well, it really is.

Now that we have covered the header of the JD, let's look at what remains. The work of any individual can be broken down into daily, weekly, monthly, quarterly, and organisational activities. There's nothing more than this. Our responsibility in creating a JD is to ensure that each part of the responsibilities that we create, is mirrored in our training program for this role. On the other hand, as we create the training program for a job role we may find that there are things that we missed out of the JD.

Through all of training creation it is essential to keep in mind that training is always a work in progress.

Job Title
Reports to
Works with
Qualities of a person in this role include:
Job summary

Responsibilities:
Daily
Weekly
Monthly
Quarterly/Annual
Organizing

And that's all I have to say about that! Don't waste precious time and resources trying to be perfect. Focus on excellence, being the best that you can be right now and producing the best possible content that you can, right now. As you learn and grow you will come back to material that you have previously created and wonder whatever you were thinking when you created it. Material has a habit of changing with age, it becomes obsolete or superseded by something better, so waiting until you have the perfect content is a total waste of time.

Learn, implement.
Observe, relearn.
Improve, implement:
Repeat

The outcome will be ever-improving content.

The JD will appear again in our Orientation Training Program.

CHAPTER ELEVEN
ORIENTATION TRAINING PROGRAM

Orientation Training Programs OTP are so important that every single time you board an aeroplane you attend another OTP. Typically the content is well presented, in a logical sequence that is memorable and interesting. It engages participants (willing or not) to auditory and visual training. Some airlines even make it fun or funny to increase the information retention rate. You watch and learn because your life may depend upon it.

The OTP at your company is just as important. You are giving every team member a detailed introduction to your business and assuring that they know and understand why they are present and what they are here to do. They discover the key team members, find out important facts about the history of the organisation and how to access assistance if required.

A good OTP is comprised of:
- Company welcome
- Story of the brand
- MVV
- HR department services- & employee handbook and Job Description
- Policies on use of phones, eating, smoking, late coming & absences (these must be covered and pointed out carefully, because they are key elements of the culture of the organisation.
- Grooming standards
- Tour of the brand
- First Aid & Fire Safety

- Social media and the brand
- The hierarchy/leadership team
- A montage of team members sharing why they love the brand.

How you present it is up to you. We recommend that the best way to ensure an exact replication of this information is delivered to every team member is that you create videos that share the messages that you wish to convey. Trainers, no matter how talented, will not be able to continuously repeat the same message with the same level of engagement and enthusiasm over and over. So take the hit, make the content, produce the videos and share them with every new team member as they join the organisation. Content is king and there are abundant creative team members who would love to participate in the creation process.

Make sure that you have an excellent OTP.

CHAPTER TWELVE
LEARNING PROGRAMS FOR JOB ROLES
SOS & SOP

Now we come to the core of the Trainer's role, ensuring that we have the correct information available for every job role within the organisation. The two key document types that guide this learning process are Sequence of Service SOS and Standards of Performance SOP's.

SOS
STORY OF SERVICE OR SEQUENCE OF SERVICE

After almost 40 years of training in restaurants and hotels I would say that the Story of Service or Sequence of Service is the most significant document the company owns.

It is in this document that we express the exact customer journey in the tiniest of details and this is probably the biggest content creation process that you will ever undertake.

First of all you must have the right people in the room to create the story/sequence of service. The right people means those who absolutely represent and uphold the concept, fully understand the customer needs, have the commitment to work hard to create the process that will guide all team members in providing a consistently excellent level of service and the perseverance to see the process through to the end. Typically these are the owners and team members closely associated with the highest levels of management.

The story of service is written commencing from the first moment of customer contact with the business to the last moment of contact. It covers every step of the customer experience that we can predict, and as we learn from our customers we expand it further and add more sessions to it.

Here's how you do it:

- Have an intelligent and experienced **note taker** who understands the operational concept and the desired customer service experience.
- Have a **narrator**, someone who is responsible to talk through the journey from beginning to end.
- Have **contributors** from each area of the customer experience that you are working on.

The narrator's job is to speak through the experience and the best place to do this is in the workplace where the role happens. If this process is done in the pre-opening stages then you will most likely be in a construction site, and whatever you produce will most likely need adjustments about six weeks after opening when the true process will become obvious.

The value of creating a great SOS must never be underestimated, for in creating the SOS you define the customer journey for every employee undertaking a role in such detail that nothing is left to chance.

The narrator will ask questions of the group such as, "Will we carry the menus with the hostess and present them to customers as they are seated, or will the waiter present the menus?"

"Will the hostess take the water order or will the waiter do that at the end of taking the drinks order?" and so on. The answers to these questions will form the SOS.

Here's what a final step in an SOS may look like:

Leading customers to their table.

The Host/ess will only take customers to a table that is clean and prepared for receiving customers. If the table needs preparation first, the Host/ess will smile and say, *"Please would you wait one moment while we prepare your table for you?"* and indicate with their open right hand a place to the side of the main thoroughfare where the customers should wait. The Host/ess guesses the approximate timeframe for the preparation of the table and adds 2 minutes, smiling and saying, *"Your table will be ready in (x+2) minutes."*

As soon as the table is ready, the Host/ess takes the appropriate number of menus in their left hand and with their right hand open, they gesture to the customers, smile and say, *"This way please."* The Host/ess then walks steadily, taking the nicest route to the customer's table, constantly checking that the customers are walking along with them, and answering any questions that customers may ask as they make the journey. The Host/ess will always be a few steps ahead of the customers.

Upon reaching the table the Host/ess will position themselves at the far end of the table and pivot to face the customers, smile and with an open right hand gesture, point to the table and smiling will say, *"This is your table for lunch/dinner today."* When there are older people and ladies, the Host/ess will assist in pulling out the chair for those customers. In the case where it is only gentlemen the Host/ess will touch the back of the chair nearest to them as a gesture.

Once the customers are all seated the Host/ess will then distribute the menus to the customers starting with children first, then Ladies, then older gentleman and younger gentlemen. The Host/ess smiles and presents the menu with their right hand with the menu facing the right way up and open to the most appropriate page (this may be appetisers or drinks depending upon where your customers will typically begin their meal journey).

Before the Host/ess departs they will smile and say, *"So and so will be serving you this evening. Enjoy your meal,"* saying the name of the server who will be the captain for the meal experience.

The Host/ess will then leave the table and return to the front desk, smiling and acknowledging customers as they walk whenever they make eye contact.

This is one step in an SOS.

Notice the number of times that it states smile or smiling! It is 8 times in one single step of the SOS. The reason for this repetition is that repetition creates mastery. Each part of the step is measurable and things like open handed gestures are an important part of demonstrating openness and hospitality.

In my experience there are a minimum of 20 sessions that will go into a normal sequence of service. These steps will define what is going to be expected from the service team while they are working and delivering customer service. While the creation process is happening it is an exciting experience that is driven by asking a series of simple questions:

1. What comes first?
2. What comes next?
3. What comes after that?
4. What do we want to see happen in each step - EXACTLY
5. What do we want our team to say in each step - PARAMETERS/EXACTLY

Once we have completed walking through the customer journey, a meeting that normally takes about four to five hours, we will have a long list of steps. These notes must be carefully transcribed into steps which will form the foundation for our training sessions.

Creating the SOS is a form of content creation and so it is necessary to invest in building the content according to the content creation standard we previously spoke of in Chapter Seven.

SOP
STANDARD OF PERFORMANCE
SOPs or Standard of Performance, are as equally important as the SOS and are a step by step guide to a repetitive technical process, given to those who are required to perform the task.

For the past few decades SOPs have remained as documents on the shelf of some office in a folder (that will be stolen by departing managers and produced in their next workplace as the best way of doing things). Time and again I have seen this take place, the problem is that the SOP's from one establishment are perfectly useless in another, and yet they are traded as currency.

In truth, most SOPs are rarely if ever referred to and are often even hard to find. We believe that an SOP is related more to product production and to non-service tasks whereas an SOS is related to the interactive and physical task of serving customers.

Don't waste time writing SOPs that are never going to be used.

The usefulness of an SOP is this: Will you measure team performance against the SOP?

IF you can honestly answer yes, and you can demonstrate the effective measurement process, **AND** introduce me to the actual measurer who is following up on this SOP, **THEN** you have the perfect background for writing an SOP. Otherwise, skip it.

No measurement - no value.

The format of an SOP has two parts, the first is general information including the SOP title, date created along with who created the SOP and a reference code. Usually it is a good idea to have a way of recording changes and the name of the person who made the changes. The second part of the SOP is the Task itself, well described, in steps, with exact standards listed out in a simple and understandable way.

Part 1: General information:
    Title of standard
    Reference code
    Creator & Co-collaborators' Names (+ Approvers)
    Date of creation & dates of revision (and by whom revised)

Materials required for this task

Part 2: Process

Task	Procedure (Steps)	Standard (What level is expected)

The combined contents of an OTP, JD, SOS and its associated SOPs should be that:

A reasonably intelligent person would be able to take these documents and by following them, become proficient at what you want them to do.

This is the proof of having done an excellent job in creating the right content for each role.

CHAPTER 13
PRODUCT LEARNING

Pictures, videos and personal experience!

Learning about the product is vital. If you are working in the Front Office and have never stayed in the hotel, how are you going to relate to the people that you are providing a product for? If you have never tasted the food and drinks you are serving, how will you be able to tell customers what it tastes like?

You must have a personal experience of everything that you are providing to your customers. Sometimes I hear that this is going to be expensive or that we are too busy to let our team members experience the product. This is complete nonsense. You have invested a vast amount of capital in creating your product, it stands to reason that the people who are selling your product must know and understand what it is that they are providing.

It should be a part of every new employee's journey to experience the product, and that cost is part of your investment. Don't cut corners on this very important step. Inviting your team members to experience the product is a wonderful step to letting them feel how important they are to your operation and helps them create memories of their own that they can share with customers. Be rich towards your team in this area and the benefits will come back in powerful selling experiences for your customers.

Every product must have a picture or video associated with it. You must show a picture to every team member of everything you sell. They must know and understand what it is and how it feels. They are then prepared to meet customers. There is nothing worse in customer experiences than being told by a server that they need to check with their supervisor.

Make product cards in a logical sequence.

If it is room types then take the time to have a photo reference of every room type and the list of all amenities that are in the room. State what the benefits are for the product and what the normal selling price is for that product. Explain the unique value of the product in such a way that it is memorable. A video of a room typical of that room type will help in building knowledge.

Menu items, drinks and wines should be explained on two different levels. The first level is for general knowledge and information, and will commence with a nice description of the product, it will mention how long it takes to serve this item to the customer from order time to table, anything that can be added or removed to or from the product, what tablewhere is required and if there is anything accompanying the item. Allergens will be stated too. Sometimes a brief description of how to create this item will be added, and it is also a good idea to have a sales script for house specials. All of this information should be available to team members. Add a wonderful picture, a hero shot, of the item.

Level 2 in product cards is the list of ingredients in the product along with the quantities and a step by step instruction on how to make the product. Taking pictures of each step or a video of the process is an excellent way to create learning experiences for team members.

As with all learning, the best test of this process is to give your product card to an intelligent person and have them produce the item from the learning card/pictures/videos.

Testing product knowledge is essential to establishing the learning process and we strongly recommend that each item is a training session in and of itself.

These form classical SOPs.

The objective of product learning is to ensure professional and smooth knowledge transfer from team members to customers in an excellent manner.

CHAPTER FOURTEEN
ADVANCED LEARNING

Levelling up.

When you invest in me I feel valuable and I perform at a higher level. There is no better way to inspire your team than to provide them with high quality learning that goes beyond their basic learning processes. Everything we have covered so far is focused on having an employee perform their work to the desired level of the operation. Advanced learning is about helping team members gain more information on WHY things are done the way that they are.

Advanced learning is designed to meet a different need from discovering general work requirements and standards; it is about elevating them to a higher level of understanding in different subjects that are related to their work.

Common topics include, but are not limited to:
- Leadership learning
- Communication skills
- Team mechanics
- Handling difficult employee situations
- Handling difficult customer situations
- Profit & Loss statements and management
- Budgeting and resource optimization
- Motivation and delegation
- Goal setting
- Time management strategies
- Coaching and mentorship

Another field of advanced learning is about products:

- Understanding the origins of wine and wine regions
- Whisky knowledge
- Coffee knowledge
- Hygiene and food safety

And so the list goes on, and is only limited by your creativity. A lot of times advanced learning is provided by an outsourced company (like ours ●). What is important to keep in mind when hiring outsourced training is to ensure that you receive from the trainers the entire course material to share with your team. This then gets compiled into advanced training programs that can be shared with new employees joining in the future.

If you do not record the advanced training programs or keep the course materials then you end up with disposable sessions that expire with time or as team members move on.

Focus on your operational needs and your team's needs and algin the advanced programs with their growth in mind. We are morally obligated to train people for the betterment of the industry, knowing that many of the people that we train will eventually move on to another company. This raises the question of, "Why bother?" My answer is, "Because we all learned things from the various courses and seminars that we have attended in the past that make us what we are today. If no one would have invested in us we would not have made the journey to where we are!"

There are thousands of online learning solutions for advanced programs too and a quick online search will yield many valuable resources. These can all be useful sources of growth for our team members, and most of them are paid for services. In order to develop our library of information for our teams we should encourage this type of growth with the provisor that the participants are going to build a learning experience for other team members from whatever they have been able to learn, and this is recorded as an advanced learning program.

Investing in your team is investing in your own success.

CHAPTER 15
VERIFICATION

In my experience, the downfall of any failed operation can be pinned on one single factor, poor managers.

No manager will ever admit to not being good at what they do, but the truth of the matter is that in our industry a lot of leaders have been promoted due to their wonderful personality and good performance at a lower role and so have been elevated to the next level, however, most often without proper preparation. This is often the consequence of an urgent need to fill a position and using the most available solution to solve that need. In order for managers to be fully capable of what they are required to do they must be taught how to do their new role. Frequently this does not happen and new managers learn by osmosis. They copy the behavioural patterns of the managers around them and repeat whatever works best. This is not a good foundation for management growth.

Where I see this most is in managers not getting engaged in training their team members. They often delegate this responsibility to others, and avoid getting their hands dirty. Managers should be the best trainers of their teams and should devote substantial time to training. They usually have the most experience of the work that is required to be done and understand it better than anyone else, and yet they are not involved in the process.

To overcome this I believe that verification is where managers can make a significant difference to the learning process.

Verification of team members by managers makes both parties responsible and accountable. In true verification a manager will measure the abilities of a team member against the information and knowledge that they should have attained for the role they are performing. If this is done properly we will avoid the risk of having people in positions for which they do not fully understand their responsibilities. By having the managers verify their team members, they are now personally attached to the performance of all of their team and can vouch for them that they are capable of doing the job to the correct standard. If this principle is practised throughout the entire organisation then managers will in turn be verified by their managers and we will have resolved the issue of unqualified people in leadership roles, for they too will have undergone a training for their role and been verified by those who lead them.

In virtually all of the businesses that we work with, there are little to no training sessions developed for managers and almost no standards for how a manager should perform. If we build our system properly, then every manager will have training sessions attached to their role and they will be verified too, assuring a higher level of managers running our businesses.

Every manager must be shown the value and importance of verifying that their team can actually do the job they have been hired and trained for and this is fairly simple to do. At the point where a trainee (at any level) has completed their standard training program their manager should undertake a face to face, one-on-one process of proving their competence. This should be a non-negotiable element of the training process.

Here's how to do it:

- Set up a one-on-one meeting with sufficient time allocated to walk through the entire process
- Have a prepared list of questions related to the job to ask the trainee - it can be written or verbal - with a prescribed list of expectations for the answers.
- Meet the trainee and go through the questions and answers methodically. Rate the results.
- Have a prepared list of "Show and tell" activities related to the standards and SOS and have them demonstrate their proficiency live to the manager. Rate the results.
- Identify areas of success and commend and areas of weakness for further training and produce a plan with a timeline for reaching success.

Through this simple and effective process we will be assured that our team is capable and professional. We will be able to hold our managers accountable for their team's performance and managers will be able to assure complete success of every team member over time.

The objective of verification is to ensure that every person working in our operation is fully capable to do their job to our standards and systematically assist wherever there is a deficiency.

CHAPTER 16
EVALUATIONS

I love evaluations.

A great evaluation is where a team member first gets to measure their own opinion of how they are doing. Their first evaluation opportunity should come once they have completed their OTP, JD, SOS and SOP training. It is at this point that they are now ready to say how they feel about their work, if they think they are now capable of doing their work and to share their thoughts. Asking new employees such questions as what they think we need to make the work-place better is a great way of discovering needs that we may have overlooked. They have fresh eyes and are new to everything in our processes and can tell us what it really feels like to be a part of our business.

The ideal time for their first evaluation is before probation is over. When the team member evaluates themselves it creates a token system that puts a demand on our managers to respond to what they have said.

This is now the moment for managers to conduct a first evaluation face to face with the new employee. This also applies to promoted employees, for they have had to learn a whole new series of standards and SOP's from the ones they had in their first role.

The manager is well equipped for this evaluation by having in their hands what the employee is thinking and feeling about their own performance, and having conducted a verification of their abilities everything is in place to assure a great conversation.

The manager must think of the evaluation as the moment of truth, where they decide if this person is in fact a good fit for the business and if their capabilities are up to the level that has been created for that role. Throughout the evaluation process the manager will be seeking to inspire the individual to want to continue their growth and to encourage a heart level commitment to the ongoing work they will be performing.

The evaluation should take place with every single employee at the end of their initial learning phase to ensure that no employee remains within the organisation that is not a good fit, and to create a memorable moment where the employee knows that they are a welcome and valuable team member.

Positive and inspiring evaluations are truthful and direct, and must be conducted with confidence and confidentiality. Recording the outcome is important, and providing the employee with a record of what has been said is essential to a successful process.

Further evaluations of all team members should be a regular part of management work and should be conducted frequently, and not less than once every six months. "Once every six months," you say? Absolutely! Waiting to evaluate team members on an annual basis is asking for mediocrity and allows issues to simmer for far longer than they should. Engaging in an evaluation with every team member every six months guarantees that you have had quality time with all of your team members at least twice a year and you and them are comfortable with how things are going.

Interim ways of measuring performance can be conducted by giving commendations and praise to your team in a recorded manner. WhatsApp is not a good way to do this because as we all know, our WhatsApp stream gets lost over time and anything good that you have shared with an employee on that platform or a similar one, just gets lost. We recommend a system of recording praise of individuals' good actions with a date and specific comments. This encourages your team to repeat the good actions that they have been rewarded for and creates a lot of good will between team members. Share the good news with everyone when someone does well.

In our platform this is a core part of managers' work and we have a part that is a simple one click commendation that ensures the good deeds are recorded in their online performance file.

Likewise, we always encourage employee feedback and we suggest that you have a My Ideas forum where team members can share ideas. This works in two ways, it provides a place for genuine good ideas that will improve the business and a place for whistleblowers to share things that are not going right. The way we recommend that you do this is on an online platform where the ideas are instantly shared to the HR team and top management. This is the equivalent to the old suggestions box that used to be in the back of house areas.

Reinforcing great behaviour
is a path to excellence.

CHAPTER 17
CERTIFICATION

Receiving a certificate is a reinforcement of my value.

When you complete the training of OTP, JD, SOS and SOP's and you have completed verification and undergone an evaluation is the perfect time to certify team members. As a frontline employee a certificate is meaningful recognition of completion of the process and for management it is an indicator that the whole process of learning the required standards has been successful.

The certification process must be automatic. Once a team member has been verified and evaluated they need to know where they stand and nothing says it better than a certificate that states what program they have completed. Having that certificate means the world to them and is good for your organisation too. They will add this to their CV and will carry that certificate for years to come, which shows that they are now competent in your eyes, but also tells other organisations to whom they apply to work in the future that you are professionals and take their job role seriously!

The certificate should have important signatures on them. The owner or senior management is the best signature that an employee can possibly receive. It reinforces to them that the senior management are aware of them, that their contribution is important to the company and that they are valued.

On the other hand, the certification process also makes senior management aware that their team members are completing the learning process and that the management team is performing their role of knowledge transfer professionally. It is completing the circle if you like. We hired a team member and now they are certified: this means that they have been trained, their manager is accountable for their performance because without verification and evaluation there is no certificate, so it is taken for granted that every step of learning has been properly completed.

No certificate?
Incomplete process!

CHAPTER 18
HOW TO TRAIN = ABC

Finally, we have reached the best part of this book and I am glad you are still with me and that you have made it this far (and if you just jumped into this book here, I highly recommend that you go back and read the preceding chapters because without them this will not make complete sense).

I LOVE TRAINING!

Training is an act of love. It is the opportunity to give to others something that you have learned and it is the ultimate reward in life. To give is better than to receive and nowhere more than in training. Watching the transformation of trainees as they learn, seeing them light up as they catch on and figure out something new, is the joy that training brings. Training must come from the heart.

Everything that we have discussed up to this point is to prepare us for what is now to come. This is a long chapter, but it is broken down into many steps. Each step has its own title and the purpose of this section is so that you can personally put into action effective and powerful sessions. Typically I take three days to train this chapter so that at the end of it, every participant can stand up in front of a group of people and successfully deliver a session that will be memorable and take the learner to the level that is required.

1. Planning

Once we have created our training content we now have the task of delivering the training sessions to our team members. A typical job role training plan will look like a checklist:

Waiter

Mission Vision and Values ■
Employee Handbook ■
Job Description ■
Orientation Training Program - OTP ■
Sequence of Service Sessions - SOS ■
Product Learning Sessions - SOPs ■
Verification ■
Evaluation ■
Certification ■

This checklist ensures that the complete content is transferred to the person in their job role and that their performance is verified, the person is evaluated and certified. Once this has been done you have succeeded in your mission.

On a digital platform this is relatively simple to achieve, because the platform will ensure that the learner has direct access to everything that they need, as they need it. Each step has a verification of completion where the learner will complete either a quiz or an acknowledgement of completion and the platform will not allow access to the subsequent step without completion of the previous one.

In a physical training program where there is no digital support one must create a Training Matrix on a spreadsheet with the list of all the sessions down the left hand side, the name of the trainee at the top of the column and then a two part process for completion and verification of learning for each session. Colour coding is an excellent way to do a manual matrix, with red indicating 'not done', yellow indicating 'trained - not verified' and green indicating 'done and verified'. It is simple and effective but requires a tremendous amount of manual work to transfer records onto the spreadsheet, and frequently becomes so heavy that training progress gets quickly left aside. This is the reason we created the platform DONE, so that you can do all of this work digitally and accurately, where each user will have their own profile and their quizzes and verification are all online and progress automatically updates their progress records.

Either way is fine, manual requires a tremendous amount of ongoing work and all training is dependent upon a trainer delivering the content live for each trainee, and then recording that training. Digital does it all for you and you can see at a glance the progress of your team with one number, total number of certified team members.

With the checklist complete we are now ready to create a plan. Digitally the plan can be specified to be completed within a certain number of days from the outset of employment or promotion, whereas with manual we have to follow up on each person's progress and schedule live sessions for every single session.

To create a manual program requires a schedule to be produced that will inform trainers and trainees of the time and place for training and then ensure attendance.

Frequently managers will declare that they do training every day, meaning that they have a daily briefing. This is not training, it's a briefing. A briefing is a short meeting where we share missing products, VIP's and special announcements for the day. We can include reminders of topics that require refreshing, and we can talk about upselling items and give company notices. However this must never be considered as training, since there is insufficient time in a briefing to cover a topic properly and ensure competency.

Training has a fixed time, a fixed place, a session plan and an opportunity for practising what has been trained. There must be an agreement about who is going to conduct the training session and an announcement to the trainee of their requirement to attend.

Training must always be conducted during working time, for it is work. Many times at the end of training sessions people say, "Ok, now let's get back to real work" or something similar. This is poor practice as it communicates a wrong message to team members. Training is the core of establishing our standards to our team and is an extremely important part of our work.

Planning training must take into consideration the mental state of our trainee, conducting training at the end of shifts or early mornings when trainees work late the night before is a recipe for failure. Ensure that training is programmed for times when trainees and trainers alike are going to be fresh and alert. If you have to schedule it on a day off, then you must be clear that this time will be compensated for so that trainees know that this is work.

Ensure that the place where training is going to take place has no distractions, and try and make the appeal of attending fun and worthwhile by providing coffee and tea.

Your plan must include ensuring that you have all the equipment necessary for the session, such as:

Projector or screen & cables (or bluetooth)
Sound system or a good speaker for sound
Flipcharts/Whiteboard & marker pens
Pens and paper
Refreshments & candy

2. Pre-Session Preparation
Before conducting the session the trainer must ensure that they have properly prepared for the session.
   a. Read through the session outline and memorise the key points/steps/chunks. Writing the key step titles on a small piece of paper can be a useful tool for the trainer. Underline any phrases or actions that participants must be able to do by the end of the session.
   b. Have a copy of the session for each participant
   c. Know who is going to attend - a list of invitees
   d. Have a training session record (or if you are using a digital process, have the sign in credentials ready)
   e. If the trainees are not known to you or each other have name cards or name badges prepared in advance. If you cannot print them, then provide marker pens for trainees to make their own name card.
   f. Prepare the materials that you are going to use in the session in sufficient quantity for the number of trainees.
   g. If you are using a presentation, make sure that you have reviewed all the slides for the sessions and that they are clear and appropriate. Go through the entire session before you start. Have a clicker to advance the slides and test it before you start so that you are familiar with how it works.
   h. Have a clock or watch - know how long the session is going to take. We recommend as we mentioned before that no session should be longer than 30

minutes. This ensures that the session content will be memorable.

i. Have your questions already planned. Write down the key questions so that you don't have to think on the spot.

j. Have feedback notes - use Post It pads for this and just hand them out at the appropriate time.

k. Prepare the space, put the notepads or paper and pens in an available space - make sure that the positioning of the participants is right for you. Be ready to move the tables and chairs if necessary to get the room to feel right for what you want to achieve.

l. Dress right - look good and get your head in the game. You must always come to training with a positive outlook and be in a smiling frame of mind. Angry trainers cannot succeed, it just ends up as a rant!

m. Be ready 5 minutes before the start of the session

Now you are ready for your session.

3. The structure of your session = A B C

A great training session has a beginning, a middle and an end. The way I do it is to create an Attention, a Breakdown and a Check.

A = Attention
B = Breakdown
C = Check

Attention = A, is getting the session started, getting the attention of our trainees and letting them know what this session is all about. In a 30 minute session the A should be not more than 5 minutes in total.

Breakdown = B, explaining the learning and conducting the actual training of the topic. In a 30 minute session the B is about 20 minutes in length.

Check = C, making sure that the learning has been effective and successful and that every trainee can in fact do what you have trained them to do, and then taking feedback from the trainees. In a 30 minute session the C is about 5 minutes in length.

By structuring your session in this way you can never go wrong. Here's how it works:

4. Attention = A (+/- 5 min)

Attention is structured to ensure that the session starts off powerfully and effectively.

     a. Welcome
     b. Training session record
     c. Title and introduction
     d. Icebreaker
     e. Purpose of the session - What's in it for me? WIIFM

   a. **Welcome** - the welcome starts before the session actually begins and this requires that you are ready to go so that you can focus on the arriving participants. Be at ease and greet every trainee personally by making physical contact, either shaking hands, or a tap on the shoulder or even a hug if you know the people well. This makes it obvious that this is going to be a good time. Once everyone is present then give a warm welcome to indicate that we are going to start

b. **Training session record** - without a training session record we consider that training has not taken place.

No training record?
No training done

Without a record of training we consider that there was no training. Thinking that we will remember who attended is useless. The training record should either be signed or digital and must be recorded at the beginning before we start doing the training. During the time when people are signing in play some uplifting music or chit chat with participants who have already signed in. Do not start the session until the vital process is complete, because if you do, the participants will be distracted and miss your important information at the beginning of the session. The training session record must record the following:

- Title of the session
- Date of the session and time
- Name of the trainer
- Name of the trainee
- Signature of the trainee

Having completed the training session record we are now ready to start for real.

c. **Title and Intro** - Begin by stating the title of your session. This makes it clear what people are here to learn. Recently as I named the title of the session one of the participants stood up and left as they realised that they were in the wrong place!

When stating the title we can also add a bit of context to the topic, stating what we are here to learn. I often set up a parking lot too, this is a blank flip chart page that I stick on the wall for people to add questions that they think of as we go along that we will answer at the end of the session. Explain how long the session is going to last. I call this:

Tell them what you are going to tell them

d. **Icebreaker** - The icebreaker is a fun start to any session and takes many forms. The objective of the icebreaker is to get people to focus on being present. Where trainees do not know each other well, you can have them introduce themselves to one another, you can ask a question and have them write down the answers, and then share the answers with other participants. You can have them do a stretching exercise, a breathing exercise or answer a cool question about something related to the topic. What is your favourite restaurant and why? Who is your favourite famous chef and why? This is your opportunity to be creative and should be planned out in advance so that it is natural and fun. Make sure that your icebreaker is relevant to the topic, fun and enjoyable and that the length of the icebreaker is short enough.

e. **Purpose of the session** - What's in it for me (**WIIFM**) - this is a statement that ensures that trainees know what they are here to learn and why. We start our WIIFM with a sentence that looks something like this: "By the end of this session you will be able to…" and state what they will be able to do, or "By the end of this session you will know and understand…" and state what they will learn. This will prepare their minds to know the outcome of the session and give them the reason why they should attend. If you WIIFM tells them something meaningful and gives a good incentive for why they should learn, the learning rate will automatically increase. Adding a live quiz at the end of a session will create a strong WIIFM too as people will pay more attention knowing they are going to be tested. Keep in mind to be certain in your statement and avoid saying "I hope". You do not need to hope, you are an excellent trainer and they WILL be able to do the task that you have trained.

These 5 elements create a tremendous welcome and get your session on track. It communicates that you are professional, know what you are talking about, and that you are prepared. Remember: PPPPP, Proper Planning Prevents Poor Performance.

5. Breakdown = B (+/- 20 min)

This is where the heart of learning takes place and in order to be successful and ensure that every trainee can do what we have trained them, we must follow a clear and structured path. I call this part:

Tell them

The structure for B is in 4 major chunks:
   a. I tell
         Ask questions
   b. I show
         Ask questions
   c. They tell me - walk me through it
         Praise and ask, "Can they do it?"
   d. They show me - do it alone
         Praise, critique, ask questions

a. **I tell** - The first part of B is to tell the participants what the task is and explain it in detail covering the topic clearly and effectively and following the steps that I have created in my planning phase. If you are using a hand out of the session, this is the best time to share it with the trainees. I now talk through the entire process from beginning to end explaining what is going on

> First...
> Second...
> Third...
> Finally

Use the chunks/steps that you have created to guide your topic, and make sure to describe well. When there is something of extreme importance you may say, "This is the most important part" and this will draw attention to this point for the trainees. Be clear what the standards are and use exact words. Read them from your sheet to make sure you are precise. At this point the participants are learning the process from you and they will remember what you have said, so getting it right the first time is essential.

Having completed my talk through the topic I then ask questions. Asking questions will give me as the trainer an indication of where the trainees are at.

b. **I show** - at this point I now go directly into demonstrating the process. You must show the trainees exactly what you want to see happen. Having used the step/chunk system during my explanation I now go into the demonstration using the exact same steps. As I go along I will say, "Firstly..." and explain the first step. By having a limited number of steps (up to 5) in my session I am certain that every trainee will be able to do what I am training. As I demonstrate I try to avoid adding too much more information than what I talked about as I told them, just sufficient to make the demonstration smooth. If I am demonstrating a process that involves people then I will select participants to be my guests. If I am demonstrating a task that has equipment, then the equipment will already be prepared and I can use it now to show them how to do it.

Emphasise the step numbers as you go along, so that they will easily remember the steps.

Having finished my demonstration I ask questions. My questions will be a recap of what I have shown them. I begin by asking, "What comes first?" and get trainees to answer the questions. I proceed through the entire demonstration by asking the trainees to tell me what comes next.

c. **They tell me** - next I ask for a volunteer of who believes that they can do this task following the standard that we have just demonstrated and I select a participant. If I have been using participants during my demonstration then I will select one of them to Tell Me the process. I begin by saying, "So, walk me through it, telling me the steps, but without doing it." I ask, "What comes first?" to get them going and then the trainee will explain to me the process. If they miss something I will ask the other participants something like, "is this the next step?" and the participants will self correct the session.

When selecting a trainee to demonstrate I always want to select someone who I am pretty certain gets it. You want to have a successful first trainee to set the pace. Never choose a weak participant as your first person because they will feel nervous and may do it all wrong and this will spoil the process. We want to have confident and positive people to start us off, let the weaker ones be near to the end of the process of demonstrating, so that they will have had the added opportunity of seeing the process repeated by others beforehand.

As soon as my trainee has completed walking me through the process I praise them. It can be a high five, or telling them, "Well done" or similar to confirm that they have done a good job. We can never praise enough. Get all the other participants to applaud the trainee. I ask them if they have any questions and generally at this point there are none.

d. **They show me** - This is the moment of truth where the trainee will now demonstrate back to me what they have just told me. I precede this with a question:

CAN YOU DO IT?

I think it is very cool to ask them this question, because their response will tell me whether they are ready or not. If they give a very hesitant, "Yes", then this is a warning sign to me that I need to double check that they are ready. Generally by now they are ready to go and I stand near enough to watch what they are doing and get them to do it. My job is not to interrupt unless there is some danger, perhaps we are using a knife or a piece of equipment and they are about to make a mistake, in which case I will tell them to stop and then ask them what they are about to do. Clarification will normally come from the other participants in a natural feedback. I ensure that the trainee does all of the steps as trained and carefully ensure that they do the exact steps as trained. I must never compromise this point, the standards must be exact.

As soon as they complete the task I tell them well done! I give more praise. Even if they did not get it completely correct, I will say, "Well done, thank you for your efforts." I avoid breaking a trainee and will then move into the next phase of training.

Critique follows praise. I ask my trainee, "How did it go?" and let them give me their feedback. If something was missed out or there was uncertainty I will follow up with, "What would you do differently or better next time?" and listen carefully to their response. I may ask the other participants, "What did you like about what/how they did that?" and let one or two of their fellow participants give feedback. Critique is a positive process of affirming what was good and what can be done better. Avoid criticism at all costs. Criticism always breaks people down while critique is focused on building people up and encouraging them to find a way to be better the next time round.

We finish up with this trainee by asking if they have any questions and now we are ready to move on to the next trainee.

EVERY TRAINEE MUST GO THROUGH TELL & SHOW

At this point the trainer must think carefully about how they feel the trainee did. If the trainee got it we move on to the next trainee. We cannot assume that because the first trainee got it, that everyone got it.

In large groups I use peer learning and have the participants divide themselves into groups and practise the session together. One person in the group is appointed the role of observer, one will be the person doing the task and another will be doing the task. The groups then rotate the roles until everyone has practised the task, and while they are doing this, the trainer will visit every group to ensure that the task is being done correctly and to the standard.

In small groups, everyone will come to the trainer and demonstrate the task to the trainer.

Here it is again:

B = BREAKDOWN

I TELL - USING STEPS
ASK QUESTIONS

I SHOW - USING STEPS
ASK QUESTIONS

THEY TELL ME - WALK ME THROUGH IT
PRAISE, ASK QUESTIONS

THEY SHOW ME - CAN YOU DO IT?
PRAISE, CRITIQUE, ASK QUESTIONS

Having completed the training of every participant and being sure that everyone can do it, I will highlight any key points that stand out to me that need to be re-emphasized.

6. Check = C (+/- 5 min)

Having completed the knowledge transfer and had everyone demonstrate the task, I now want to be sure that the task is locked in. I do this by checking. Checking is as much for the trainer to confirm that the training is successful as it is for the trainee to have a review of the topic. I call this part:

Tell them what you told them

The structure of C is in 4 main parts:

    a. Praise
    b. Review and Confirm
    c. Link
    d. Thanks, feedback and sign out

    a. **Praise** - yes, again! The more praise and positivity in the session the more you promote a good feeling about being in a training session. You also cause people to feel good about themselves and we know that people who feel good, do good. So, as you go into C you begin with praise. "Well done everyone." Be genuine and sincere and look at people while you say this. Try to avoid highlighting anyone as the hero trainee and direct your praise towards everyone.

    b. **Review and confirm** - this is a very important part of the process and it is in this moment that you are establishing in your own mind that your trainees really got the process. Start by declaring a review of the session, open room questions and selecting different participants to answer, begin with step one and work through the steps of your process logically from beginning to end. Ask the participants for the key learning points and praise good answers, and get others to help when answers are slightly shaky. Your review is solidifying the learning into their minds and preparing them for action. Now is the time for a quiz if you have planned on giving one. The best way to do a quiz is to ask the questions out loud, have the participants write the answers and then swap their papers with other participants to check. You then review the questions out loud and have participants share the answers and grade the papers. This way you will have completed all of the grading in a swift manner. If there are any questions in your parking lot, this is the moment where you answer them. Take each question one at a time and ask the question to the room and see if the participants can answer them. Give your opinion or answer to the question and if you cannot answer it, promise to come back with an answer (and do so).

Only move on if you are sure that the topic is understood. If you have some doubts about the learning you may decide to have a follow up session on this topic. If you session descended into chaos, and sometimes this happens for unforeseeable reasons, stick to the plan. Keep on going and complete your C, but decide to redo the session again very soon with corrections in place.

c. **Link** - this is where you connect your participants to some further learning in the future. If you are training on a sequence of service then you will tell them the time and place for the next session. This will make a sub-conscious connection for the trainee that this information is important and must be retained and assists in creating a long term memory. Your link can also be to a practical test of their learning within their working environment.

d. **Thanks, feedback and sign out** - You must close up your session by thanking your participants for their attendance. You may hand out your feedback notes at this time for trainees to share with you one thing they learned or a thought on the session. On our platform they do this digitally, but writing it down on paper is a great way to do it too. Collect and read the feedback and take note of what was said.

Ensure that all trainees sign out of the session before they leave and you are almost done.

Hang around after the session for a couple of minutes. You will have some clearing up to do, but you really want to make yourself available for people to come and talk to you. This is when you will receive your "Trainer's reward", the gratitude of your participants, and where they will feel confident to ask you questions. Avoid being busy with other things during these moments, they are important and it is nice for you to get personal comments from your trainees.

And that's it! You've trained your people.

CHAPTER NINETEEN
QUESTIONS

In order to enrich your sessions you can add plenty of texture to the learning process by mastering your techniques. What follows in this section is a collection of useful things that I have learned throughout my training journey and I want you to know them. If you have some of your own that you think should be included there then kindly share them and we will add them into our book (and mention your name of course!).

a. **Questions** - I love questions. You can have an entire conversation with someone and they will think you are awesome just by asking questions and listening to their response. I believe in:

AQAL
Ask Questions And Listen

By asking questions and listening we become better informed and the person we are speaking with has a sense of being heard. This creates a great relationship with that person. While they are answering your question:

STAL
Stop Talking And Learn

Frequently while people are talking we are busy thinking of what we are going to say, rather than listening to what they are saying. Allow yourself to listen to what they are saying and learn from them.

A pause after they have spoken is good and let's people know that you have listened to them. Thank people for any questions that they ask you, "That's a great question" or "Thank you for asking" and cool responses can be, "I had never thought about that" or similar.

Through this method you are positioning yourself as an intelligent conversationalist and often you will end up not even talking about yourself. Most often when we are speaking we are repeating things that we already know, while listening allows us to acquire new knowledge and information. The questioning method also allows people to verbalise things and by doing this it can sometimes straighten out their thoughts and cause them to put them into words. A very useful thing.

All trainers have a series of familiar questions that are great for getting sessions going. Beginning with "Why are you here?" is one of my favourites because it shifts the focus from the trainer to the trainee and they have to think about the reason why they are present, or doing what they are doing. Another question that can get a session going is, "What do you want?" and getting the participants to write down three things they want. This can be a broad question or focused on the specifics of what they want to get out of this session. I almost always follow this question with, "When do you want it?" and again I get them to write their answers. You can have participants share their answers with the person next to them to get people talking (a great ice breaking exercise).

Closed questions - there is no such thing as a bad question and closed questions, though often shunned by some are a great way of building. A question I will always avoid is, "Do you understand?" because this question will almost without fail produce the answer, "Yes". A far better question is, "What did you understand?" as this causes the participants to share a more elaborated answer. "Please explain what you understood" is an even better question because it gets participants to go even deeper into their answer.

I use closed questions to build confidence or to create an affirmation from the participants as a group. "Are you ready?" and listen to the sound of the answer. If you get a few mumbled yesses then you need to crank it up. Say, "No, no, no! I asked, Are you ready?" and participants will automatically raise their energy level with a stronger response. If the response is not yet at the level that you are seeking I then get them to stand up, stand strong and then ask again in a loud voice, "Are you ready?" and the participants at this point will give a much stronger response. This question technique builds the energy in the room and gets the participants to experience a rush of dopamine.

Sometimes I make a statement such as, "Are you with me? Yes or no?" and the participants will automatically answer, "Yes" and again if this is not strong enough as an answer I will repeat, "Yes or no?" and they will again elevate their response. Through this simple but effective way you are creating a personal commitment to what is going to follow as people say, "Yes" they refocus.

Discovery questions - "Can anyone tell me about...?" By asking this kind of question I can get various different participants to volunteer information. I often use this question near the beginning of my sessions. It helps me to know the level of knowledge of my participants. I always avoid having people say how they have previously done the task that we are discussing, because I do not want them to share a wrong process, or a process that I disagree with, I want to have my participants' minds focused on my content, so try to avoid this. The objective of discovery questions is to find out what people know without tainting the training that is coming up.

Confirmation questions - in this type of question I am looking for a confirmation of what I have trained. Key words in confirmation are explain, demonstrate and show and may look something like this: "Why can show me?" or "Who would like to explain this?" and then listen carefully for the information you are seeking to confirm.

Direct questions - I use these questions by asking the name of the person that I specifically want to answer the question. "David, please would you tell me what you think about…?" In this question type I am getting a focused answer from a specific person. I want to know this person's answer.

Helping questions - when a direct question does not deliver the right answer, or indeed any answer I use the technique of asking the person to the right of the one to whom I asked the original question saying, "Can you help?" If they are unable to answer I will go to the person on the left hand side of my original target. This allows the person who was originally asked to feel with the people around them and does not make it so pointed that they were unable to answer.

Open room questions - When the answer to a direct or helping question did not elicit a good response I open the question to everyone, using open hands I say, "Can anyone help?" or "Does anyone know?" Sometimes I will say, "Ok, let's ask Google. Check on your phones..." and this will find the answer. By using this three part technique we are able to impress on our participants that not knowing the answer is not the end. Everyone joining together in finding the answer encourages the team to grow closer together.

PPP - Pose, Pause, Pounce - in this technique we ask a question into the room without choosing anyone, then we let it hang for a second and we then pick someone to answer. This type of question has the effect of building focus among the participants as it signals that anyone may be the target for the question, so all the participants remain focused and ready for the next question, not wishing to get 'caught out' by not being ready. It's a wonderful technique that elevates attention.

Surprise questions - When we are training we may observe someone losing focus or being distracted, or doing something other than our session. In this technique we will just throw out the question by saying something like, "isn't that right, John?" and the target will look up surprised by the question and look around them unsure of what to do because they were not focused. You may say mid-sentence, "Wouldn't you agree, Peter?" and again they will have a similar response. If they were concentrating they will be able to answer and everything will proceed smoothly. If they are unable to answer we can gently suggest that they should focus in on what we were saying and then revert to the helping technique by asking the person next to them the same question, but this time framed as a question. This is a powerful way to say, "Pay attention" without actually expressing it that way.

Wrong answers - In my experience there is never a fully wrong answer. Even if the answer is totally wrong we can say, "Well thank you for your answer, it's not what I was looking for..." and then go back to the helping or open room technique.

You can practise your question technique in many different settings so that when you are up in front of your trainees you will already be familiar with these styles and proficient in using them.

CHAPTER TWENTY
BODY LANGUAGE

Body language - again, there are thousands of books written on body language so here I will just focus on a few that are very effective to use as a trainer.

Open hands and correct pointing - when we are in the training environment we use our open hands with palms facing upwards to point or show something. This technique taps into our limbic system, nothing hidden: nothing to fear. Open palms are a sign of friendliness. Pointing with our index finger is an aggressive approach that immediately signals instruction or an order and causes listeners to subconsciously put up a defensive barrier, which is something that we want to avoid at all costs. Practise pointing with your open hand, palms up.

When explaining during training try not to hold things in your hand. If you are using a clicker, put it down when you are not using it. Avoid having a marker pen in your hand unless you are writing on the board. You avoid creating distractions or the appearance of something in your hands.

Using both of your hands wide open and arms outstretched is another warm and welcoming gesture that makes people feel drawn in, invited in and can only help to add to a welcoming training session.

Stance - When we are training we want to communicate from a powerful stance. Standing slightly to one side of the room with our feet at shoulder width apart and firmly planted shows confidence and strength. You will also not get tired, as your weight is well distributed through both legs. Try not to move around too much while standing and then consciously go to the opposite side from where you were standing and take up a similar stance. This prevents you from becoming part of a fixed scene that over time will become boring for the participants. By moving around you create interest. By hopping around in one spot you show weakness or lack of confidence.

Walkabout - One of the techniques that I use is to create a different speaking spot by walking in and among the participants or by walking to the back of the room away from the screen and front of the stage and all the time I am moving I am continuing my presentation. This takes a lot of confidence in knowing your material because as you walk you are totally disconnected and so you must be able to maintain the connection. As you move to a new spot everyone's attention will be immediately drawn to where you are now and this has the effect of elevating their focus on what you are saying. This is not to be done all the time, but from time to time and normally in a longer session.

Touch - you may touch participants on the hand and shoulder and this is a technique that I use all the time. The physical touch should be so light that the participants almost don't notice that you did it. However what it will do is create a very special connection between you and the participants and it helps to build trust. Now of course, there are always going to be cases where you must not do this, but in a general training session it is very useful and appropriate and adds value to the session. I often touch the participants during group exercises by touching them on the shoulder and saying, "Great idea" or "What do you mean by that?" and their attention will be on the topic, but the connection will be made. Another time I specifically use touch is during the coffee breaks where I will tap people on their forearm while conversing or I will re-shake their hands using both of my hands, the second hand coming on top of the handshake to solidify the connection.

I like to create moments where participants touch each other and my favourite way to do this is to get everyone to stand up and give 5 hugs. The response is amazing - you have sparked oxytocin and they feel the instant reward.

Have people turn to each other and shake hands with one another and hold the handshake. Then have them say something like, "You are amazing" to the person with whom they are shaking hands. Again this triggers an amazing energy boost and creates smiles and warmth.

Using touch during training is a powerful way to get teams to bond with each other and with you as the trainer.

Down to up - use your hands to show things growing or improving. Start with your hands down and say first, then raise the hand to a higher position for the second point, then to a higher position for the next point and so on. This creates a visual connection for participants. It is as though you are building an unseen object, which will always start from the bottom and go upwards.

Left to right - demonstrate a process using your hands, starting from the left side with the first step, then move towards the right for the second step, then the third step and finally end up on the right hand side to show the last step. Left to right is logical and reinforces what you are trying to teach. It is a visual hook for participants.

You can combine down to up and left to right when you are taking them on an imaginary journey from something that was, to something that is. Start down left (which is where the old thing was, or the bad thing was) and build up from down left to top right (where good things are). Up is growth, right is right. Combining them together creates a visual pattern that we are leaving something old behind and moving up to something right and new.

Fingers and hands - You have five fingers (I guess you probably noticed that by now!) and as a trainer these are great tools for creating an anchor. Attaching a step or a chunk to a finger or to your whole hand makes things more memorable. For example, if there are five steps, hold up your open hand palm facing the participants and say, "There are five key points in this process." They will immediately associate with this. Then you hold up your thumb and point to it with your other hand and say, "First step" and name the first step. Then as you go through the process you subsequently use each of your fingers until you reach the fifth. Once you are done you are going to be able to hold up your hand and ask what the first, second, third, fourth and fifth ponts were just by pointing to your hand and participants will be able to associate with it. You can even say, "Ok, so put up your hands, what is the first point?" and get them to do the same exercise. This creates a simple anchor for them to associate the learning process to.

There are so many ways to use body language in training, sometimes I have people act out words, such as boring, angry, tired, focused and happy. As they act them out so their bodies will emulate those thoughts. Move from negative emotions to finish on a positive note and you will be able to show them that their thinking will determine their body language, and that they can command an emotion if they just think about it. This is powerful body language that helps build up a training session.

Finally you must be aware of the body language of your participants and make adjustments to your activities and speaking depending upon what you are seeing. If the participants start to get distracted and tired it may be time to call for a break. Keep on practising your awareness of body language and over time it will become a natural skill that will enhance your training.

CHAPTER TWENTY ONE
BRAINSTORMING AND
GROUP ACTIVITIES

Brainstorming and group activities - in training there is nothing more stimulating than the group activities, for it is here that we cause people to teach one another from what they already know, to create something new that elevates everyone's learning. Successful brainstorming requires excellent direction and follow up by the trainer. The first part is to give a clear brief on what is expected and the second part is to set a clear timeline. The timeline is a very special part of brainstorming or group work. We can adjust the timing as we go along making it either longer or shorter depending upon how people are doing. A short mini-group work exercise may have 40 seconds, such as, "OK, you have 40 seconds to come up with the top 3 reasons training is important, work in groups of 3. Go!" and then everyone will very quickly start to work together. If you start the exercise by saying this task has ten minutes to work together in groups of four, then the groups will form and the pace will be much more gentle.

Try to avoid creating who is in which work group as much as possible. This way you will cause the participants to figure out who will work with whom and the groups are then accountable for who is in their group because they chose.

Your role as the trainer is to go around the groups while they are working and check on them. Ask questions about how they are solving the problem. In a ten minute task you let them work for about 4 minutes and then begin your journey around the groups. Avoid giving the answers, yet give helpful suggestions or challenge thinking. After about 6 to 7 minutes you will be able to gauge if they require more time for the exercise or if you need to start closing it down. In the case where they need more time, at 7 minutes you will announce that there are still five minutes to go. If you want to wrap up the task then you will say there are 2 minutes to go. Then after about 40 seconds you say that there is about a minute remaining. Then after about 40 seconds you say 15 seconds remaining and then count down the last few seconds. This works very well in managing the time. When the workshop is an hour, then you start the first time signal at about 20 minutes, and then 15 minutes, then 10, 5 and 2 minutes. These are not real minutes, they are just sounds that indicate to participants a rough guide of how much time is left so that they increase their productivity accordingly. Have the group present their answers on flipchart paper so that it is visual and easy to present.

When a group has finished their work there will be a summary of what was learned by the group. This can be done in many ways. The first and best way is to let the groups decide who will go first.

Let the first group present without interruption and at the end ensure that there is a round of applause. Generally applause is weak and lazy. This is your opportunity to lift up the energy level and you encourage another round of applause with full energy to encourage the first group. Normally one person will speak while the rest of the group will stand around with the odd intervention. We then get all the groups to do their presentations and as the groups progress, we get more of the same. Be patient and let them all finish, each with enthusiastic applause.

Your big question here is, "So, what did you learn?" This is an open room question and you listen to them all the answers. Then you send them back to their groups to have everyone participate in presenting the material in a powerful and memorable way. This causes the groups to rethink their answers, chunk their learning points and represent them with energy and commitment.

Another way to do this is to take the flip chart presentation from each group and give it to a different group to present. This is fun and causes a higher level of learning as the groups try to figure out the material and create a way to present it as a group, involving everyone.

Group work does two key things, it creates peer to peer learning and encourages collaborative learning. Both of these methods are superior to lecturing.

If you ask the groups to present "the purpose of training", they will develop a wonderful list of reasons why training is valuable, and the learning will be far richer than the trainer going through a list of pros and cons of training.

When you are planning your training sessions you must allocate time in your plan for these group learning activities. It is always better to overestimate how long they will take than to just count the actual number of minutes for the exercise.

CHAPTER TWENTY TWO
OTHER STUFF

Other stuff - here are a collection of useful tips that I have discovered while training. I am sure you will find them useful.

Dealing with over-talkers - these are the participants that have all the answers to every question and who constantly interrupt to share their own point of view. You will not notice them at the outset of the session, but as the session goes on you will notice that they are preventing others from participating. Here's what I do: "Hey, I need you to let others answer please". This will give a kind warming to the talker. If someone is really disruptive I will ask them if they really want to be here. When they answer no, then I ask them to leave. This may seem awkward, but the rest of the group will appreciate it.

If the over-talker does not get my message then I may jump to a group exercise or call a break. During that time I will go and catch the person that is causing the issue and ask them to let others take more of a role. I may compliment them on their knowledge or let them know that they are more aware of the topic than others and that I will ask them to assist me further on in the training. Generally this will solve the problem.

Using a break - if the session is getting a bit stuck or tiring, I may call for a break. When I call for a break I know that it is not going to be less than ten minutes at the least, so I announce a seven minute break, or a 9 minute break, or I say you have five minutes and forty seconds for a break. Participants immediately figure out that this is a quick break. When it is lunch time I normally agree with the group on the return time, and I always start on time. Breaks are a moment for a trainer to regather their thoughts and review their notes for the next part of the session. As I have already mentioned, it is also a great time to bond with participants and get some instant feedback. I often ask, "How is it?" or "How are we doing so far?" and listen and watch the feedback. This will be a good indicator of how I am doing and I can adjust accordingly.

Use the break to make sure that you are comfortable and don't forget to drink a lot of water. As you speak you will exhale a lot of fluid so it is essential that you replenish your fluids often and much more than you would in a normal day.

"Fine." - this is a great word for signalling the end of something. You can wrap up a segment or a discussion using the word 'fine' and move on to a new thought.

Pauses & silences - I like to use a pause or silence during training. When the session has been going for some time and I have been talking extensively on a topic, I sometimes just stop and look out at the participants and stay quiet. It's really powerful. Everyone will look up and there will be a moment where there is almost discomfort. They are willing you to go on. The best moment to use a silence is right after a lengthy dissertation on a topic.

The pause creates attention, the silence gives time for absorbing what has been said. I may say, "Write down what you understood from what we just discussed." and then remain silent while they do that.

Remember, as the trainer the participants are dependent upon you for what comes next and they do not know your plan. So, even if you are pausing because you have lost your place, they don't know. Next time you are speaking, try it out!

Music - Have your own playlists. Some for fired up moments, some for casual moments, background music, thinking music, spiritual music. I save all my playlists on YouTube and just sign in from the device I am using to access all my music.

During the arrival and pre-session part, I play jazz or popular songs from a current playlist. During a fired up part of the event, like hugging exercises, I use rock music or great hits. When we are doing brainstorming exercises I put background music. The idea of having music is to remove the uncomfortable silences that tend to come while people are sitting in the room doing something where they may be feeling self-conscious.

Here's a perfect way to use music. I do an exercise where everyone writes down the things that they are grateful for, and I get them to write down at least seven things. While they are doing the writing I have inspiration music like the gladiator soundtrack or Enya. Once they have completed their list then I crank up a great song and have them all read out their gratitude list, loudly while the song drowns out their voices. It's awesome and creates a memorable and happy uplifting moment. Never underestimate the power of a good song to change the mood in the room.

Training and learning - not class - By this I mean that you are a trainer, not a teacher. Your role is to inspire the participants to want to absorb the material and to learn. There are no sticks, only carrots! Always lean towards being fun and inspirational rather than the serious and drudgery of school-like memories.

We will - this is a statement that comes from NLP. We plant this in the minds of our trainees by saying, "We will learn..." or "We will be able to..." The power of using positive words always causes the participants to feel like it is certain that they are going to be able to succeed. One of the phrases I use is, "You are going to have a great time today." This subconsciously tells the participants that they are going to have a great time, and sure enough, when you ask them later how it went, they will normally repeat, "It was a great time!"

Keep the training language secret - We want to avoid saying things like, "Now we are going to do an icebreaker." It's weird and people don't know what you are talking about. These phrases and our language is for us as trainers to know what we are doing and where we are in our program. Like every good magician, keep your tricks secret!

Visualisation - one method I use at the end of an intense session is a visualisation technique. I get everyone to sit quietly and take in a few deep breaths. I put on some spiritual music, softly in the background and then I talk through all of the steps that we have covered in the session and ask them to imagine themselves doing it. I walk through the entire process, explaining the process as though we are actually doing it live. At the end I ask them to open their eyes and share how they feel about it. It always has an incredibly positive impact and participants feel calm, centred and capable of doing the task. I will wrap up with a question such as, "Who feels that they are sure they can do this task?" and everyone will raise their hands.

In order to use this technique well, you should practise it yourself first.

The most important thing - Can they do the task? Your role as the trainer is to be sure that your participants can do the task that you set out to train. Until you reach that point you are not yet done. Use the tools of verification, evaluation and measurement along with our Training Needs Analysis tools to see that we have achieved what we set out to do.

If you are in doubt about the efficacy of your session, then make a note to do a follow up session or a refresher training session in the near future to review and revise what has been taught and to ensure that it is being implemented correctly. One of the ways of doing this that will keep the sessions fresh is to select the most proficient trainee to give the next session along with you. You will lead and mentor them through the session, but the actual training part will be conducted by them. This will involve that individual in practising the process or task and memorising it to be able to teach it to others. So in this process we have the opportunity to elevate our team's skills once more.

The best way to know if training is effective is to see if it works when you are not present. If your team adopts training and are training other team members without your involvement, then you have succeeded in your mission. If this is not yet the case, then you will need to create training sessions for your managers on the material in this book so that they will carry the flag forward and translate this method to their teams.

The best training programs are perpetual. You finish one round of training and then you are ready to start again from the beginning. Keep it fresh by getting team members to do it.

Management training is very important and often overlooked. By creating training programs for managers and scheduling them well in advance you will ensure that your leaders are growing and learning too.

CHAPTER TWENTY THREE
VIDEO LEARNING

With the vast amount of online content available and the growth of AI we are able to learn virtually anything online, from how to take a gearbox for your car to pieces to how to play the piano. There's a video for everything.

I believe that we are going to enter into a world of 3D AI training and we are working toward that, where all your business software will collaborate together to show you your strengths and identify areas for growth, and you will be able to meet those needs using your own material and avatars.

The quality of AI videos is exceptional and is growing rapidly. The biggest challenge with videos is knowing what content to feed into it.

Having learned how to create content you are prepared to make your own videos and this is the best way to share all of your OTP, SOS steps and SOPs. You can produce a short video for every session and save it on a platform for watching by your team members. This means that you will only have to do your training one more time personally, which is the time you make a video. Thereafter you will be able to share the video with your team members and they will learn from the video.

This elevates the importance of verification. If someone has watched a video and practised what you have trained them, the remaining part is to make sure that they are actually capable of doing what they saw in the video and so this will always remain the role of a manager. Making sure that the team members can do the job.

Here's how we make an effective video

- Write it — create the video content
- Test it — talk it through with someone who understands what is supposed to be learned
- Fix it — make adjustments as required
- Film it — We will talk about this below
- Share it — Get the video to the team
- Use it — Measure performance against the standard trained

Filming the video is so simple these days. Every smartphone has a good enough camera for filming training videos. The most important thing about shooting the video is sound and to make sure that you have great sound you will need to invest in a bluetooth microphone. These are relatively inexpensive and a good one to buy is from the Rode brand. Try to get one with two microphones so that you can record two people speaking in your video.

Every video you shoot has a similar format that goes like this:

a. Intro
b. Welcome
c. Title and topic
d. WIIFM
e. Breakdown
f. Summary
g. Closing
h. Outro

a. Intro - this is a two to three second clip of the logo of the brand with a background jingle. This will be played on every video and becomes a signature of your videos. You can create this using AI.
b. Welcome - start your video with a bright smile and say, "Hello and welcome"
c. State your name and the title of the session
d. WIIFM is all about what the watcher is going to learn - remember to tell them why
e. Breakdown - this is where you tell and show the session, covering the key points. You can add subtitles and headers to your videos as well as highlight key points on the screen
f. Summary is where you recap quickly what has been learned through this video
g. Closing - "Thank you for watching and we look forward to seeing you in our next session"
h. Outro - this is a two second clip with the logo and a jingle to signify that the video has ended.

If you follow this format your videos will be great. They take practice and my one advice is to delete every clip that you reshoot so that you don't end up with hours of bits and pieces that you don't recall what they were for. It sounds easy but it is not.

Alternatively you can call us at DONE and we will be happy to come and help you shoot your videos!

CHAPTER TWENTY FOUR
CONCLUSIONS

Training is an awesome activity and one of the most important that you can undertake in your operations. It assures excellence and over time becomes the one path to creating outstanding customer experiences.

I would love to come and train with your management team and this book is the outline of our three day 'Train the Trainer' program that has been our most successful program ever. This program changes lives and changes our world.

If you want to change the world, become an expert trainer and the only way to do that is to practise. Keep on doing it, over and over again. There is never a bad training session. You can learn from every experience and keep on getting better and better.

Remember this:

GIGO
Garbage in, garbage out.
Greatness in, greatness out.

When you make amazing training sessions you are causing people to behave differently and better. Give it 100% and focus on making 100% of your customers happy, 100% of the time.

APPENDIX 1

SESSION LISTS BY POSITION

HOST/HOSTESS

1. Welcome to Reception - Understand the reception and reservation area
2. The first contact - answering the phone
3. Handling reservations & confirming reservations
4. How to speak on the phone & how to repeat the most important things as though it is the first time you say them!
5. FTG (First Time Guest) policy and preparing data for the service team
6. Welcoming our guests
7. Seating our guests
8. Leaving the guests at the table in the care of their server
9. Assist with basic orders such as water
10. When there are guests waiting while seating others
11. Walk ins when available tables & what to do when no availability
12. Difficult questions and answers
13. Dress code violation and how to handle it
14. Lost and found items
15. Valet parking validation and how to handle them
16. Transfer of guests from table to bar and opposite
17. Guest departure - saying goodbye

BARTENDER

1. Introduction to the bar
2. Stock filling, Inventory and ordering
3. Mise en place for garnishes
4. Customer side of the bar - set up
5. Glasses and types, washing & care of glasses
6. Display and cleaning
7. Mixing
8. Blending
9. Stirring
10. Shaking
11. Building
12. Pouring
13. Welcoming customers - banter
14. Get to business - the drink
15. Serving the drink - presenting your creation
16. Customer follow-up and feedback
17. Payment and leaving
18. Closing the bar

SOMMELIER

1. Welcome to the wine department & what it means to be a sommelier
2. Meet our wines!
3. Your wine tools - waiter's friend, cloth
4. How to set up for wine service ice bucket prep, wine lists (clean etc)
5. Orientation for the glassware and glasscare, wiping fine wine glasses and storage
6. Using Coravin machine
7. Checking the inventory and par stock
8. How to approach a guest and assess what type of wine and what price category
9. How to shift between wines when selling... from expensive down from lower price up
10. Opening the bottle means you own the bottle... no one else can touch it
11. How to open and serve Champagne
12. How to open and server red/white/rose wine
13. How to decant a wine and which wines we offer to decant and which MUST decant
14. Pouring wine
15. Topping up wine... how to create an ambience of wholeness that leads to more sales
16. Serving a second bottle of same or different wine for same guests
17. Digestif sales - awareness and suggestions
18. Disposal of bottles and ice buckets and wine equipment and closing the shift
19. How to use the POS and the table numbers and table plan
20. Closing the relationship with your guest at the end of service

WAITER - SEQUENCE OF SERVICE

1. Prepare yourself for service
2. Prepare your side station
3. Prepare the condiments
4. Polishing cutlery
5. Polishing glasses
6. Folding napkins and handling napkins
7. Check your station and your work area
8. Ready to receive your guests
9. Welcome the guests at the table - Get their experience started
10. First Time Guests - FTG
11. Getting the drinks started
12. Taking the food order
13. Serving the drinks and building the atmosphere
14. Clearing the empty dishes and preparing for the main course
15. Delivering the main course - the star of the meal experience
16. Instant follow up for pouring wine and selling more drinks
17. Make sure the manager passes and touches my tables
18. Clearing the main course and dropping the hint for dessert
19. Brining the dessert menu and selling desserts and coffee
20. Serving the desserts and coffee
21. Awaiting the guests' request for the check or anything else
22. After the check and saying goodbye
23. Clearing the table, checking for left items and resetting
24. Closing duties of a waiter

HOUSEKEEPING

1. Introduction to Housekeeping, what we do, guests, entering their rooms and respecting privacy and security
2. Service orders - learning about your work for the day
3. Cleaning a toilet & setting the toilet paper and toilet amenities
4. Cleaning a sink & setting the soap, lotion and amenities & towels (folding)
5. Cleaning a bath/shower & setting the shampoo, gel, lotion, amenities & towels (folding)
6. Cleaning the general bathroom area (mirrors/floor/etc)
7. How to strip the bed
8. Handling soiled linen from the bathroom and the bed
9. Making the bed, including mattress protector, sheets and duvet
10. Pillow management and pillow slips
11. Preparing extra beds/cots/cribs
12. When & how to turn the mattress
13. Cleaning of the general surfaces in a room, including the closets & drawers
14. Cleaning mirrors, windows and screens
15. Use of the vacuum cleaner and basic maintenance
16. The guest laundry cycle
17. How to handle lost and found items
18. Public area assignments - corridors & elevators
19. Public area assignments - public restrooms
20. Public area assignments - care of furniture, amenities, cleanliness
21. Basic maintenance items that everyone should know (Light bulbs, wear & tear, paint care)
22. Awareness of security and safety and how to handle suspicious people and/or objects

FRONT OFFICE

1. Introduction to the Front Office
2. Talk about the layout of the hotel, distribution of the rooms and explain all room types & room rates
3. Welcoming and greeting a guest at the Front Desk
4. Telephone etiquette - building exceptional guest relationships on the phone
5. Guest notes - introduction to Guest History & how we collect data, why and how we use it
6. VIP notes, codes and amenities
7. Credit cards and how we handle them
8. Check in procedure
9. Upselling
10. Check out procedure
11. Enrolling guests into our rewards program (if available)
12. Handling guest special occasion requests
13. Handling guest room inspection requests & conducting a room orientation
14. Handling guest messages, parcels and deliveries
15. Handling requests for local activities bookings
16. Handling transport requests/taxi/online app etc
17. Handling guest luggage - on check in and check out
18. Managing & assigning rooms on the system
19. Escorting guests to their room
20. Handling changes to guest reservations
21. Updating guest history
22. Payment receiving, paid outs, billing and customer finance
23. Handling room moves for guests
24. Handling credit limits
25. Handling currency exchange

CONCIERGE

1. Introduction to the Concierge, what we are, what we do and why we do it - the proud tradition of Crossed Keys "Les Clef d"Or"
2. Welcoming & greetings guests
3. Escorting guests to their room and showing the room
4. How to receive tips elegantly and how to avoid appearing as "wanting" a tip
5. Handling guest requests at the concierge - General information about the hotel and local area
6. Handling guest requests at the concierge - Taxi & transportation requests
7. Handling guest requests at the concierge - Messages (receiving for and from guests)
7. Handling luggage on arrival and departure
8. Collecting luggage and items from guests and for guests
9. Handling lost luggage
10. Managing the luggage store, the concierge desk drawers and the storage of important information
11. Using digital devices to assist guests
12. The importance of guest confidentiality

QUALITY ASSURANCE

1. Welcome to the Quality Assurance Team - explanation of roles and responsibilities and the overall objective of this team
2. Introduction to specific checklists and procedures and the timetable of implementation

STEWARDING PROGRAM

1. Welcome to the Stewarding Team - the heart of cleanliness and support
2. Introduction to HACCP
3. Washing & sanitising your own hands before anything else
4. Chemicals and chemical awareness
5. Sanitation checking protocols & sanitation of all surfaces
6. Managing the dish washing process - receiving used items - Decoy system
7. Waste segregation
8. Breakage control
9. Garbage clearance
10. Floor care - washing and cleaning
11. High pressure washer - floor and wall cleaning process
12. Chopping board colour codes, cleaning & storage procedures
13. Heavy equipment cleaning procedures - mixers, slicers, boilers, ovens, fryers, grills etc
14. Handling waste oil for disposal
15. Electrical equipment cleaning procedures - microwaves, mixers, convection ovens
16. Trolley cleaning and sanitation
17. Pots & Pans cleaning and sanitation
18. Food storage area cleaning & basic safe food storage procedures
19. Knife handling & safe sanitation and storage of knives
20. Inventory, counting and equipment control responsibilities

KITCHEN ESSENTIALS

When considering building a training program in the kitchen there are some essentials that must be there. Here are our recommendations:

1. General kitchen introduction and outline of the structure of the food production team
2. How the kitchen team communicates - hierarchy & expectations of team members
3. Personal hygiene, grooming and uniform basics
4. Introduction to HACCP, chemicals for cleaning & recording of incidents
5. Chopping boards & knives and color coding
6. Washing & sanitising hands
7. First aid for cuts and burns
8. Fire safety & what to do in case of an emergency
9. Receiving and storage of goods
10. FIFO usage policy
11. Labelling of food items & tracing
12. Food allergens for Chefs
13. Basic knife skills
14. Principle cooking methods
15. Cooking & reheating
16. Food safety storage temperatures
17. Usage of heavy machines - industrial fryers, ovens, grills
18. Usage of slicing machine
19. Usage of vacuum packing machine
20. Responsibility towards waste and garbage management in the kitchen

ENGINEERING/MAINTENANCE

1. Welcome and the importance of the role of engineering
2. Engineering trades available on site & those supplied by contractors (including how to connect with them)
3. Work assignment system - receiving, assigning, progress tracking, completion and reporting
4. Health & safety at work - respecting all legal requirements for Health & Safety at all times
5. Planned maintenance - scheduling & implementation
6. Emergency procedures - Fire, electrical fault, coordination with authorities in emergencies, floor plans and fire alarm system
7. Basic equipment storage for repairs and maintenance - inventory/ordering/storage
8. Basic tools availability, storage and maintenance
9. HVAC management, handbooks and policy
10. Electrical team responsibilities
11. Technician responsibilities
12. Plumber responsibilities
13. Carpenter & mason responsibilities or contractors
14. Facilities daily checklist by discipline and overall

FINANCE

1. Welcome to the Finance Team and general overview of the department and responsibilities, including Functions of Finance Team (in-house and outsourced)
2. Compliance and Data Protection policies explained
3. Cash handling procedures, money management, tips management
4. Reporting requirements

SECURITY TEAM

1. Welcome and introduction to the security team - structure & reporting system
2. Basic security practices in the workplace & description of our guest type, what to expect in an ordinary guest
3. Security of property
4. Security of people
5. CCTV management
6. Signing in and out of people - knowing how many are on premises at all times
7. Theft and control by team members - right to search with respect of personal rights of individuals
8 Theft by guests - managing theft by customers
9. Conflict management - Fighting customers - handling & engaging with local authorities - use of force
10. Guest screening techniques at key security points & general surveillance - incident reporting

HR & LEARNING TEAM

1. Welcome to the team and overview of the roles and responsibilities of the team
2. Employee welfare overview and the rights and responsibilities of employees - employee handbook
3. The hiring process - talent acquisition guidelines and policy
4. The onboarding process
5. Uniforms and equipment distribution & receiving back
6. Employee termination process
7. Employee learning responsibilities and process of learning

APPENDIX 2

ORIENTATION VIDEO LIST

1. Welcome to the brand by the Founder. In this video we aim to have approximately 2 minutes that include images of the brand and the Founder speaking about the brand Here is another example of a tremendous opening video https://youtu.be/GR7YxoRh5zk

2. Country welcome. When the brand has many team members that come from other countries to work here, we provide a welcome to the country and explain important points about culture and working in this country

3. The story of the brand - our history, DNA In this video we tell the story of how the company started, key milestones along the way and what makes this brand special

4. Our Mission Vision & Values - Our Way of Doing Things In this video we tell the Mission with an explanation about it We talk about the vision for the brand into the future We share the values and what makes them important to our future growth

5. The HR Department Services Here we explain how to get your employee contract We explain where to get the handbook and the Job Description We explain the different kinds of leave and where to obtain the forms to apply We explain the salary and payment process If the organisation offers advances or loans, we explain the terms and conditions

6. Answering the phones, smoking, meals, late coming & absence and mobile phone usage These are the 5 most important points that an employee must know

7. Our grooming standards The overall grooming standards are defined, often with images of what great grooming looks like

8. Tour of the brand This is a video that takes people on a

tour of the location and shares the most important features of the brand's location

9. First Aid & Fire Safety

10. Social Media of the brand and what we can do on social media for the brand

11. Introduce the senior leadership team (desirable not essential) Short introductions by the senior leadership team of who they are and welcoming team members on board

12. Why I love the brand This is a video made from short clips of different team members expressing why they love the brand

13. Tell us what you have learned This is a 15 second video that introduces the concept of Live Verification and then there is a live verification for this session that asks questions about what has already been learned

LEARNING OPPORTUNITIES

We conduct **'Train the Trainer'** multiple times each year and in different parts of the world. The minimum number of participants for the program is 8 and there is no maximum number. Our biggest TTT program was over 50 people at one time. Our programs are like rock concerts. This is always a three day program.

We also have other very well know programs such as

Sell like a Rockstar - a one day program that grows sales

MDP - Management Development Program - this program is for anyone in management and is focused on growing management skills. There are 24 learning hours in this program which can be taken over three days, or split up over a longer period. There is a textbook that we have written that accompanies this course.

Executive Development Program - this is a one-on-one program that we have developed for CEOs, General Managers and others in senior leadership roles. Each course is customised according to the needs and level of the participant. These programs typically take three to four months and involve regular sessions, all of which are live.

DONE.FYI
Done is registered in the UAE and our offices are located in Dubai.

www.done.fyi   +971 52 452 3339
info@done.fyi

www.ingramcontent.com/pod-product-compliance
Lightning Source LLC
Chambersburg PA
CBHW062313290526
45794CB00005B/1790